life

after

you

hayley grace

Я

life after you

copyright © 2024 Hayley Grace. All rights reserved.
life after you
ISBN: 979-8-218-57237-2

no part of this book may be reproduced, distributed, or transmitted by any means without the prior written permission of the publisher. for information, contact the publisher at: contact@reldamedia.com

life after you

for anyone who lost themselves
loving somebody else

life after you

sometimes, when you're in a dark place, you think
you've been buried, but you've actually been planted
— christine caine

contents

during you	9
between you	39
after you	81

1

life after you

my head knows that it's over
but my heart won't believe it.

i've tried to convince it a million times,
but it's like trying to tell a kid
the tooth fairy is still real
after they watch their mom
slip a five dollar bill under their pillow.

my heart still believes there is magic.
my heart still believes that *you* are magic.

but behind even the greatest magicians.
there is always a trick
and yours was the greatest of them all.

"sleight of hand" is what they call it.

you use your left hand
to interlock your fingers between mine.
while using your right hand
to text other women that embody everything
i am not.

i know the tricks you have up your sleeve.
but maybe if i pretend i don't.

then our fingers can stay interlocked
a little while longer.

i almost begged.
the last time we spoke.
almost let the words slip from my tongue
"please, love me."
but instead the taste of blood filled my mouth,
as my teeth sank into my tongue.
and yeah that was painful, but it hurt less
than me begging another man to love me
and him looking me in the eyes telling me
he can't.
i *almost* loved you
and you,
you *almost* loved me.
but my head stopped my heart before it could,
because it knew you were only temporary
it knew you were going to abandon me.
leave me, like the lost toys hidden in your attic.

i *almost* begged
but i didn't.
because i am tired of begging people to love me.
and being left in return.

so that's it.
it just ends.
our story ends before it could ever begin.

almost.
that's all we would ever be

an *almost* beautiful
and an *almost* tragic story.
but always
just an *almost*.
i've had many "almost" some-things.
but you,
you will always be my favorite.

―――

life after you

if i close my eyes hard enough
i still see the man you were when i met you for
the first time.

maybe this is why i keep hitting "snooze" on
my alarms.

because if everytime i wake up
you are no longer the man i met in the beginning.

you will still exist in my dreams.

we still exist when i close my eyes

―――

life after you

"we're just friends"
he says after he cleans the dna from himself
off of her stomach.

"i know"
she replies, as her smile starts to fade.

but was it all really this casual?
because i didn't know *casual* meant
wiping my tears away with your left hand,
while using your right to push my hair
behind my ear.

was it casual when you told me
about your family?
and when you let me confide in you
about mine?

i told you that
just because my home was broken
didn't mean that i was too.
was it casual when you told me
you had never met anyone like me before?

was it casual when you stripped the clothes
off of my back
and told me the scars that hid beneath them
made me even more beautiful?

is this something friends do?

why am i ashamed of myself
for not seeing the signs,
when there were no signs in the first place?

"we're just friends," he reminds her again,
for what would be the last time.

her skin goes pale
while her eyes begin to swell,
and she whispers
"then why did you take me to dinner?"

―――

life after you

we have endured rocky waters
sailing coast to coast.
through treacherous storms
and unsafe conditions.
some i thought might leave me dead.

we have finally made it to the harbor,
and i'm safe here.
there are no unfamiliar paths,
and we don't encounter dangerous weather.

i wonder what it would be like
to sail through the water again.
but the unknown is what keeps me tied to shore.

storms have entered the harbor now,
and it's been months since i have seen the sun.
i'm afraid of the water.

afraid i won't make it out alive.
if i try to leave.

but ships were not built for this.
ships were not built to rot in this harbor.
and i'd rather drown
trying to sail through the water
than never see the sun again.

will i make it out alive?

———

life after you

i'm a ghost in our own home.
when i walk in our house,
he no longer greets me at the front door.
i've gotten used to the silence.
the pictures that hang on the walls
hold only memories
of what we once were.
i feel just as invisible now as i did when i was 7,
trying to stop my parents
from breaking glass
in the kitchen.

i guess i'll just haunt this house too.
———

life after you

moths are so stupid.
they are attracted to something
that could kill them.
they will continuously chase the light
even if their life is what's on the line.
but they are fighters.
they don't give up.

you're lying on the bed of your
childhood bedroom,
staring up at the light in between the blades
of the fan.
and you watch the moth repeatedly throw itself
into the light,
mistaking it for the moon.
you are watching the moth slowly kill itself,
as it collides with the glass bulb.

am i no different than the moth that's flying in
my bedroom?
continuously chasing someone
that is going to take the life out of me.
fighting for a chance that someday it will
be different.
and this lightbulb that i'm constantly throwing
myself at
will someday be the moon.
i don't know why i do it.
i know my actions will eventually
have consequences.

life after you

i know he will never be who i want him to be.
so why am i still fighting?
why do i fight to be seen?
heard?
touched?
loved?
if i know *love* will be the thing that kills me?

before i went to bed that night, i turned my
light off.
i hope the moth stops mistaking my bedroom light
for the moon.
and maybe i'll stop mistaking the
love i deserve,
with *you*.

―――

life after you

i've never been a rule breaker.
i had straight a's in high school,
cleaned the dishes before dawn,
and showed up 30 minutes before my curfew.
i stopped at stop signs,
never went over the limit.
and always said "please" and "thank you."

i sat in his car most nights
a secret i was told to keep.
i kept it well because i don't
break the rules.

rule #1: *never fall in love*.

he held my hand,
only in the dark,
but he rubbed his thumb
back and forth on the side of my hand.
it was nice.

we talked till 11pm most nights,
listening to old indie rock,
before i asked him to bring me home,
just 30 minutes before my curfew
because i didn't
break the rules.

i'd blush when he'd call me pretty

and laugh at his ignorant jokes,
because he said it was cute.
he talked about his family
and told me his house was made of glass.
while i told him my father burned ours to
the ground.

our lips locking each time before stepping out of
the car.
knowing i'd be back here again tomorrow.
nocturnal like bats,
our souls live in the dark
and never in the light.

but i'll accept it until tomorrow.
when i tell him i am a rule breaker

because i think i just broke rule #1

———

life after you

i can see the storm that's headed our way.
the alert goes through my head
everytime you check your phone,
and place it face down
on the counter.

i know it is coming
but i'm not sure i have prepared well enough
for it.
i know we won't make it out together.
i just hope

i make it out alive.

in preparation for the pain

———

life after you

you liked the color red,
so i carved your name
into my wrists,
watching the blood drip to the floor.

you liked fruit,
so i spread my thighs giving you the
forbidden one,
and let you scrape out my insides,
letting you consume every last drop.

you liked devotion,
so i worshiped
at the altar of your existence.
sacrificing my hopes and my dreams.
every prayer, a whispered promise to be
everything you wanted,
everything that you needed.

you liked fire, so i took the lighter to my skin,
letting the flames consume my identity.
hoping the ashes would form something
you might actually want.

even if there was barely anything left of me,
i hoped that you could find something
worth wanting,
in the residue that was left of the person
that i was.

life after you

and with the small fraction
of my brain that was left,
and that still belonged to me.

all i could hope
was that red was still
your favorite color.

———

life after you

i've never been much of an addict.
sure, i'll have the occasional cigarette once and
a while
and drink some champagne on the weekends.
but i never did drugs.
it was never my thing.

so why is it,
that you give me millions of reasons to leave
but everyday i wake up
in your navy blue sheets on the left side of
the bed.

you didn't lock the door.
you're not holding me hostage.
there is no electric fence
keeping me from leaving you.
but every time i reach for the knob on the
front door,
i turn around
before i can turn the knob.

most addicts don't admit to having an addiction.
and maybe that's why i've stayed for so long,
when i know i should have left.

parents warn you about nicotine,
and alcohol,
and drugs.

but they don't warn you about *love*.
they don't warn you that sometimes
having a love addiction
can share qualities with a drug addiction.

like that day you look in the mirror,
and you don't recognize the person
that stares back at you anymore.

send me to rehab
———

life after you

i'd rather stay with you in this broken house,
with the shattered windows
and the door that creaks,
from the countless times
you've slammed it shut.

than buy a new "welcome" mat
with someone else.
who still has to learn my favorite color.

i'll wait until you rebuild our home

———

life after you

but "i love him"
i tell my mother.
as she uses her fingers
to wipe away the droplets
from my cheeks and my chin.

"tell me what you love about him?"
she asked me.
almost like this is a hypothetical question.
almost as if she truly believes
that i can't name something about him
that is loveable.

"i love the way *he* makes me laugh,"
"the same way i still love him"
"when *he* makes me cry."
"i loves his hands,"
"for the way they wrap themselves
around my waist."
"the same way i love them"
"even after he raises them at me
when we fight."
"i love his voice,"
"the way he whispers in my ear
before i fall asleep."
"and i still love it."
"after he uses it to scream at me
after spilling milk on the counter top."

"i *love* the best parts of him,"

"the same way i *love* the worst parts of him."

"mom you just don't understand."
"i would still love him,
if he did not
love.
me."

i love the "hatred" inside of him too
―――

"love you."
he says before he steps out the front door.

"love you *more*."
i say to myself, standing in the kitchen.
after he shuts the door in my face.

there's a difference.
i will love him behind closed doors.

and he can't love me
while they are still open.

i win the "i love you more" fight
———

life after you

my heart has been locked up
in a human-sized cage.
bound by fear
afraid to break free.

like a bird.
trapped in a cage
with a door that's wide open.
her wings give her the freedom to fly away.
explore new horizons, see new skies.

but there she sits,
clinging to familiar bars.
although the cage confines her,
she feels safe in its familiarity.

and although the sky is clear,
and she can hear birds chirping in the distance,
it all still seems so uncertain.

the bird's wings ache for flight.
but fear and comfort keep her grounded.
so in the cage she stays,
hidden from the rest of the world.

i don't want to hide for the rest of my life.
i want to set myself free.

*leaving the cage won't kill you,
staying inside of it will*

———

life after you

you *used* to hold me with love.

you still do
hold me,
but only with regret.

you turn over after leaving your dna
on my stomach,
and you only touch me in the dark.

you used to love me with the lights on.
and say my name
like it was the only word you knew in english.

this room is nothing but
an abandoned alleyway.

cold and quiet.

what happened to all the lights?

———

"what happened to our plans?"
i scream at him from the bottom of the staircase.

"and the big white dog, and the two story house."
"you said you wanted to be the father of
my children!"

he looks down at me breathless, with wide eyes.

"wanted,"

his voice cracks back at me.

"that was then. but that is not now."

and for the first time,
i do not recognize the man who stands in front
of me.

something died that day.

and i'm afraid it will haunt me forever.

i think you will haunt me forever

———

life after you

"why don't you leave him?"
my father utters at me from the kitchen.

"you always come home crying."

"do you think mom's father asked her that too?"
"do you think he asked her that about you?"
i reply back with running mascara and a
raspy voice.

"well your mother and i were diff-"

and before he could finish his sentence
"nothing is different.
it is exactly the same."
i screeched back at him.

"i can't leave him
because he looks
just like
you."

i see my father
in every man i meet.

and in every different version,
they are all still
bitter.

———

him

i set her on fire,
and pretend to wonder,
why is she burning?

i want to watch
her turn to ash.
cold and small.

i want her to run back,
like i'm the only person
who can put her back together.

i get off on it.
it makes me feel whole.
it makes me feel worthy.

when i put her pieces back,
i'll cut her
with the glass.

so that she remembers me *forever.*

just so i know,

she will always come back.

———

her

he sets me on fire,
it must be an accident.
he won't let me burn.

it was an accident,
he will put the fire out.
he won't let me burn to ash.

i ran back.
he is the only person
that can put me back together.

he loves me,
he makes me feel whole.
he makes me feel worthy.

he put me back together
but he scraped my arm
with a piece of the glass.

but i know he'll love me *forever*

and he knows,

i will always come back.

———

2

between you

i'm so jealous.
and it's so utterly embarrassing
to admit this out loud.
but i am so jealous of the women
you get to love after me.

because when i met you,
you were everything but gentle
and soft and tender.
razor blades for fingers,
every place you touched me made me bleed.
scars that still live inside of my brain,
from every harsh word you threw at me.
and i still stayed.

i let you lay me down on a fucking table,
and open me up just to show you
that my heart was only beating for one person.
and that one person was you.

i showed you that no matter how many times
you tried to break me, i could still be soft.
i showed you gentle love,
even when i didn't have any for myself.

i know love exists because i am full of it.
and i gave it all to *you*.
and now i'm jealous because
you stole the one thing that belonged to me.

life after you

you stole my love
and now you get to bury it in somebody else.

i hope she knows how much violence i suffered
in order for her to be loved gently.
i wonder if she knows it isn't you
she's fallen in love with.
it's *me*.

it's all my love.
i wonder if she knows you're a fraud?
i wonder if she knows
there is a warrant out for your arrest?
for stealing all the *best parts of me*.

the next time i fall in love
i'll do better research,
to make sure there is no woman in his shadows.

because there always is
a woman who lives
behind
a man.

———

you say you will find me in every lifetime
but,
you cannot even find me in this one.

you speak as if i am lost
and cannot be found.

but i am right here.

*it's not a game of hide and seek
if i'm not hiding.*

———

i'm a recovering addict.
and no it wasn't alcohol, or drugs, it was you.
the addiction to loving a man who does not know
how to love correctly
is substance abuse.

and you were fucking *poison*.
the bruises on my body may have faded over time,
but they left scars on the insides of my brain.
like an itch that never gets fucking scratched.
the lingering.
oh god, the lingering.
is this why i crave such intimacy, but i am so
deathly afraid of it?

afraid of the next time a man raises his voice
at me,
his fists are what follow shortly after.
it's easy for you to forget about me,
but it's hard to forget you when i'm flinching after
some guy reaches over my knees
just to grab something from his
glove compartment.
his fucking glove compartment.

when a stoner needs something stronger because
he doesn't get high anymore,
he smokes a lot more weed to reach that same
level of high.

every time we fought it built that tolerance, and i
needed something stronger.
because little fights resulted in little reward.
but throwing me into walls
and bringing me flowers the next day
gave me a new high.

and you knew i'd never leave, because you knew i
was addicted.
loving you was the drug
that stayed infiltrated throughout my veins.
the residue is now trapped within my body
and will *always* live inside of me.

now i'm in recovery,
looking in the mirror at a girl whose eyes were
once swollen shut.
who used concealer to cover the bruise marks
where kisses should have been placed instead.

and after all of that i'm still soft.
what is this obsession i have with broken glass
and angry people?
i may have grown up in an angry household,
but i didn't realize that i'd grown up to love the
people who made it angry in the first place.

was it my fault?
because i stayed?

because i let you take the light out of me?
because i kept handing you the knife that was
slowly killing me?
and cleaning up my own blood
from this red-stained carpet,
just to cover your tracks?
hoping that one day there would be kisses where
these bruises lay?

they tell kids from a young age to "stay away
from drugs"

i should've listened to my mother.

―――

life after you

sometimes the hardest pill to swallow is
letting go.

because how do i let go of something
i don't even think i'm holding onto anymore?
i'm not holding onto *it*–
it is what's holding onto me,
gripping me like a little kid grabs their
mother's hand
when they have to get the flu shot.

gripping me like the last time i held the person
i loved,
when we both knew it was over.
how do i let go?
how do i let go of the things
that don't hold purpose in my life anymore?

when they have camouflaged themselves
to live in the depths of my brain
and behind the veins in my heart.
because everytime i think i'm letting go,
and unraveling the rope that's tied to my body,
it gets stuck around my feet
and drags behind me like dead weight.

the things i want to let go of
constantly follow me everywhere i go.
i can't get rid of them.

life after you

the harder i try,
the longer the rope stretches.

i'm afraid i won't ever be able to fully let go
of the things i once loved so deeply.
i guess i'll just have to learn
to grow around them
and build myself to be stronger.

so that the dead weight that follows me around
doesn't feel dead anymore.

―――

they say when one door closes another one opens.
so why am i standing in front of the first door?
screaming, crying, begging.

leaving claw marks on the hinges.
why do i stand beside it with a crowbar,
attempting to pry it back open
over and over again?

it's like i'm trying to prove a point to everyone
that i am not weak.
i can get this door back open.

i wanna go back,
back to when you didn't change the locks
and the code to the door was our anniversary.

i don't want to give up and walk away.
i want to walk back in,
in through this door
just one more time.
please just one more time.

what if i don't like what's behind the other door?
what if it's not safe?
what if it's uncomfortable?
what if i open the new door,
and you aren't standing behind it to greet me?

life after you

moving on is so hard,
when you don't know what comes next.
but it becomes a lot easier
when you realize you shouldn't be trying
to pry back open a door
for a person who shut it on you in the first place.

―――

life after you

i don't know how i could've been more.

i let you steal the clothes off my back,
just so you would stay warm.

the same way i let you take my innocence,
when it was never yours to take in the first place.

i kept letting you take, and take, and take.
until there was nothing left of me
but a mere shadow.

the numbers started dropping from the scale,
as the hair fell from my head–

i was crazy.

that's what you told everyone, after you left me in
the burning house.

but you got off on it.
because you knew i wasn't really crazy.
i was really just crazy for you.
and you needed me.
you fed off of me and the ego boost i gave you.
every time you slammed the door in my face.
i stood there like a beggar.

begging you to want me for more than the fruit

between my legs.
i begged you to look at me
like i was worth something.
like i was important.
like something you never wanted to lose.

instead you just kept asking me
if i would die for you.
but everytime you knew my answer,
before i could slip the words off my tongue.

you knew my answer would have been *yes*.

you kept asking me if i would *die* for you?

and all i kept wondering was,

why do you want me dead?
____

life after you

if i had nine lives
i'd spend the first one drowning
feel the water seep into my lungs,
stealing my oxygen and stripping my breath.

maybe after i become unconscious
i'd find peace
and i would no longer fear the ocean.

i could spend the rest of my 8 lives living by
the water, living with no fears.

for my next two
i'd spend each one with my parents.
live in their shadows, learn their deepest
secrets, and listen to their regrets.

just so i don't fuck up lives 4 through 9.
i'll hold their hands gently and watch them
take their last breaths.

in my fourth life i'll run away.
i'll run away from myself,
the person i can not change
because i am still too naive to understand
that i am all the things that are wrong with
me.

i'll chase butterflies and try to find myself.

life after you

ill look in all the wrong places, wrong cities, wrong people.
and before i know it i've ran through 3 of my 9 lives.

in my 7th life i'll listen to my parents advice,
i'll work a 9-5, make a stable income
settle down with a man i'm not sure i'm in love with,
but he is a good father to my children.
we will have a white picket fence, red door, and a big fluffy dog
one that barks at the mailman.

for my 8th life i'll live it alone.
ill write books,
live in a little apartment in new york city,
spend my days writing in a cafe around the block from where i live,
and drink wine before bed.

i'll do yoga, eat clean, and have an occasional cigarette off my balcony.
i'll raise a cat by myself
and he will watch me take my last breath before my last life.

in my final life
i'll look for you.

life after you

i'll wait at bus stops,
move back to our hometown,
try and find you at shitty dive bars,
and write letters i'll never send.

i'll realize that after living 8 lives,
something was missing
going about life without the person i loved,
made it all seem meaningless
but i don't have 9 lives
i just have this one
so i guess i'll spend it
sitting by the ocean
and
waiting for you

―――

life after you

i gave you all of the best parts of me,
but you still chose someone else.

i dropped everything for you.

for your calls.
just to hear your voice.

i left my plans early
to tend to your needs.
because you made me believe
they were mine too.

because you made me believe i *needed* you.

i spent hours of my day laughing with you on
the phone.
i felt like a little kid again.
and you told me you did too.

i would have thrown my life away
i would have put my dreams and aspirations
in the back of my back pocket.
if that was what it would have taken

for you to choose me.

i would have dyed my hair,
cut my hair,

life after you

lost weight,
gained weight.

i would have quit my bad habits,

all of them *except you*.

if that was what it would have taken
for you to see me as something other than
broken fucking glass.

but everytime i asked for more
you told me you could only give me less.

and i stayed, hoping you would change your mind.

and one day you did,
you really did change your mind.

you showed up,
and you gave more.
and you stayed.

all for a girl who was *not* me.

―――

life after you

what did she give that i did not?

what did she give you
that you thought
i was so beyond incapable of?

i know it can't be time, because i gave you that.
i gave you all of it.
actually, i gave you roughly 500,000 minutes of
my time.

enough time for the earth to orbit around the sun.

you were my light.
you were my sun.
my world constantly revolved around yours.

you said you weren't ready to settle down.
but i still built you a temporary home to keep you
dry from the rain.

and you liked it.
i mean you had to have liked it because
you stayed.

you may not have unpacked your things,
but you still stayed.
even if it was
for a little while.

until you moved out, and moved in with
somebody else.
this time unpacking your things,
putting your toothbrush in the same cup holder
as *hers*.

and i know i don't have red hair like her.
but you told me you liked my soft brown curls.
and my big brown eyes.

you told me i was different.
you told me *we were different*.

and no i don't have emerald eyes like she does.
the type of eyes anybody gets lost in.
and no i don't have a body like her.

but i have a body like me.

and that–

that should have been *enough*.

i hope you give her the life that you dreamed of
giving me.

and i won't lie, and say i hope it goes well,

but for you,

life after you

i can only hope

that it will be enough.

———

my card declined at this restaurant the other day.
and instead of asking me if there was someone i
could call,

they made me sit there.
and stare.
at the empty chair,
and the empty plate.
the untouched fork that was longing for someone
to pick it up.

the waiter came to the table,
eyes glued to the glass in front of me.
he poured a diet coke with lemon.
your favorite.

the waiter told me you would be joining
me shortly,
but it's been years.
and i'm still staring at this empty fucking chair.
and the same diet coke with lemon, that doesn't
have bubbles in it anymore.
and the same stupid fork that's gone untouched.

i'm glued to this chair.
frozen.
in time.

i know you're never showing up,

life after you

because you never did before,
and i know you won't start now.

so why am i still here?
when can i leave this fucking restaurant?

and even if you did show up,
and the chair was no longer empty,
and the fork was no longer lonely,
and the waiter came by to refill your diet coke for the fifth time.

you wouldn't be the same person i fell in love with when i was 16.

but for some reason
i'm still sitting in this chair.
waiting at the restaurant,
for you to save me.

please bring me cash

———

life after you

it was a disaster,
beginning to end.
we would never be infinite.

i wanted us to be.
i dreamt of it sometimes,
but deep down i knew.
everytime i looked at you
i'd stare at the hourglass above your head.
counting down the minutes
before you would destroy us.
i built you a home.

actually no.

no i didn't.
i didn't build you a home.
i grew one
inside of my body.
for you.
to save you.
to save you from everything evil in this world.
but i always knew it would never be enough.

i thought i was the sun.
and you were the rain.
and combined we could have had a
beautiful ending.

life after you

i looked for the light at the end of the tunnel.
i searched for the rainbow i thought we
could create.

but maybe i was wrong.

i thought i was the sun.
but maybe i wasn't *your* sun.

i was just a home for you.
a place to wait and stay warm.
until you could move in with someone else.

i don't think bricks could have saved us
from the storm that you were.

so i guess i gave myself away,

to the disaster it was
to love *you.*

what a disaster it was to love you

———

life after you

i blocked him on everything.
well i mean on snapchat, and
instagram, and tiktok, and facebook too.

but i didn't block his number.
obviously for *emergency* purposes only.
or for the slight chance he wants to come back.
but i'm done with him, i promise.
only if my promises hold as much truth as his did.
like when he promised to love me until he took
his last breath.
so i guess my promise doesn't hold as much
substance as i wanted.
but i won't text him first.

i'll wait,
till he misses my laugh,
or the sound of my voice,
or my stupid dad jokes that are only funny
when they come out of my mouth.

i won't text him.
but i won't block him either.
i'll keep the door closed,
but i won't lock it behind me.
i won't tell him where the key is,
but maybe i'll just leave a note.

incase

life after you

he comes back.

so he has some clues on where to find it,

i'll keep this house clean,
i'll buy a welcome mat,
i'll paint the door,
i'll build the porch.
the one we always talked about.

just in case.

but i promise i won't text you first.
i won't delete your number,
and i'll shut the door behind me too.
but i'll leave a note by the mailbox,
because if i want to make a grocery list with anyone,

it will always be
with *you*.

―――

life after you

if i could sit at the kitchen table
with my 6-year-old self
i'd tell her she was right.

monsters *are* real.

but stop looking under your bed,
because you won't find them there.

and they aren't ten feet tall, with big teeth and sharp claws.
they aren't hidden in your closet behind the shoe rack.

sometimes the real monsters
are the people you ask
to check under your bed
before you fall asleep.

sometimes it's the boy
from your 8th period math class
in the 12th grade.

and sometimes you won't even realize
it's a monster
before it's too late.

don't look for the monster under your bed.

sometimes the monsters are the people you love.

the people you will fall in love with.
the person who will hold your hand
and guide you through parts of your life.

the real monsters walk beside us everyday.
above ground, in the daylight,
hidden behind a mask of the person they pretend
to be.

maybe i shouldn't tell her.

i think if i sat at the kitchen table
with my 6-year-old self,
i'd hold back the truth.
so that maybe she has a couple more years
of believing that the scariest monsters
are the ones hidden under her bed.

and not the person she says "i love you" to
before she goes to sleep.

i loved you as the monster you were

———

how is it possible to miss you
for longer than i've known you?

it's like i hopped on this train
of the five stages of grief–

denial.
he just needs space, he'll come back

anger.
what a waste of time, he never cared

bargaining.
maybe if i do things differently, he'll come home

depression.
there is no life after him

and acceptance.

except i forgot to get off
at the last stop.

i've been riding this train,
glued to this seat,
between pain and sadness.
stuck to depression
forgetting about acceptance.

life after you

how do i stop the train
―――

life after you

why didn't you fight for me?

for us?

it's like you threw me in the ring,
just to watch me fight myself.

you were always going to leave.
you just wanted to *watch* me
beat myself up first.

i came out of this fight
a loser.

with black and blue eyes,
and i lost you too.

how are your hands so clean?
___

life after you

i used to love summer,
sand sinking beneath my feet,
warm breezes embedding themselves in my skin.
cold ice cream on hot days.

now when summer comes around, i think
about *you*.

the sand no longer sinks beneath my feet.
instead it sucks me in.
deeper and deeper into the ground.

my hands clawing at the ground, trying to keep
myself above it.
stealing my oxygen.
the same way you used to take my breath away.

we were never *something*,
but we were far from *nothing*.

hovering over the line between lovers and friends.
i always wanted more.
you knew it too.
but i would have rather been a background
character in your story,
than to not have appeared in it at all.

i loved you.
it never needed to be said,

life after you

and it never was.

because you knew.

every summer you take my breath away.

but this time,
it's not yours to take anymore.

i hope that one day,
when someone asks me
what reminds me of summer,
i can say good ice cream on hot days,
instead of *you*.

when did summer get so cold?
———

there's been a robbery and you are the culprit.
stealing my heart from my chest.

i'd call it violent theft but you'd argue
petty crime.

robbing me of my heart, soul,
stripping me of all the love i had left to give
to myself
and the person that comes
after you.

there's nothing left inside of me,
but i can still feel it pulsing and breaking even
though it's just a phantom limb.

the echo of its beat, getting louder and louder, but
the rhythm is becoming faint.

the silence inside of me may seem sweet, but the
pain is what overbears.

with every pulse, a whisper of your name.
reminding me of the thief who took the best parts
of me.
it's a ghostly throb inside of my body getting
louder and louder.

make it stop.

life after you

i want to make it stop.

this wound may be unseen, but the absence of my heart makes me incomplete.

i know i'm not bleeding, but a part of me wishes i was.
so you could see the damage you have caused,
the damage that can never be fixed.

just give me back what was mine in the first place.

give me back what was never yours to take.

you stole my heart leaving me hollow,
and now i have to wear this phantom limb.
leaving my insides with only a shadow.

i didn't know absence could hurt this deeply.

i guess i'm left with this phantom pain.

where the ghost of my heart
will remain.

———

life after you

i've been looking for you,
four long years of searching,
sitting, patiently waiting.

hoping you would return.
you made a promise you would always
come back.

even if we got lost along the way.
you made a promise that it would always be me.
but now i'm knocking on doors,
putting up signs,
a missing persons' poster on streetlights at
every corner.

sending out search dogs that use your big t-shirt
you left here four years ago
to guide them.

but they don't,
find you.
and they won't
because it's been four years
and i've slept in that t-shirt every night.

so the dogs just lead themselves to my
front porch.

no one has

life after you

seen you
you are gone.
part of the reason i can't find you
is because i don't know your scent anymore,
and i don't know what you look like now.

does your heart still beat the same?
does your pulse still speed up when you see one
of those big fluffy dogs?
do you even like dogs anymore?

i've stopped the search party.
i can't keep looking for someone
who does not want to be found.

i guess i'll just think about you
on your birthday
and wish for you back on mine.

and wonder if your favorite color is still blue?

or if all of the little things
have changed
about you too.

―――

life after you

i never really finished grieving you.
actually i'm not sure i ever really started.

i just found ways to comfort it,
the grief.
i gave it a home,
let it stay a while,
kept it warm.

swallowed it
and chased it with a bottle of tequila.
inhaled it,
let it fill my lungs through every cigarette.

i drowned it in darkness, hoping it would fade.
but it thrived in the shadows, growing darker.

i carved it into my skin, trying to bleed it out,
but it seeped into my veins, becoming a part
of me.

i tried to suffocate it with pillows of denial,
but it found its way into my dreams.

you.

found your way into my dreams,
turning them into nightmares

life after you

i fed the grief
with my fears, hoping it would choke,
but it devoured them.
the grief grew stronger with every bite.

i woke up with it, and carried it to work,
years on my back.

but it's too heavy now.

i can't move.

it holds onto me.
follows me like a shadow,
gripping my ankles.
i can't move forward,
but i need to.

i guess some shadows
never fully fade.

hopefully i won't carry this grief with me

forever.

―――

life after you

i wish i could sleep forever.

i wouldn't have to spend the days
faking my smile.
pretending i still want to be alive.

without you,
the oxygen leaves the room.
i scrape the corners of the floor,
just to find somewhere i can finally breathe.

i still see you in my dreams.
we have a life.
we built a future
there were children.

but then i wake up.
and every night before i close my eyes,
i know i'll have to live a nightmare.

because none of it is real.

you are *not* real.

i'd rather sleep forever
and see you in my dreams.
than wake up
and live without you
at all.

3

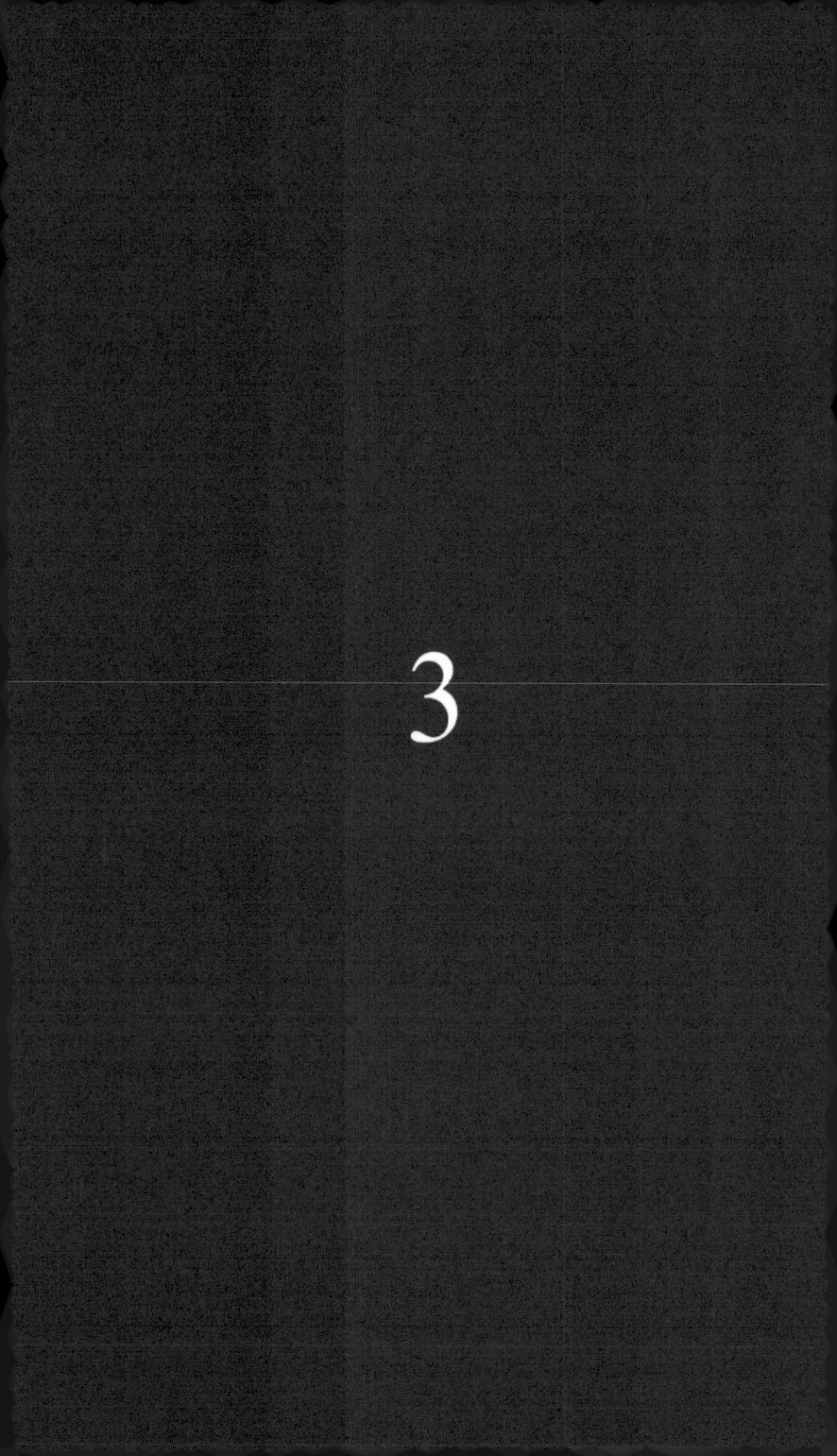

after you

the fear of being alone
left me.

the day i realized
that i cared more about me
than you ever did.

i don't need someone
to hold my hand
everytime i fall.

i learned to walk
so that i could stand up,
and keep moving forward
even when no one's beside me.

the weight of needing someone
disappeared the moment i realized

i am enough.

life after you

sometimes i wonder if i will
ever fall in love again.
but then i wake up
every morning and i do

when i saw the smile on my sister's face when she
got accepted into college.

and then a couple hours later, when my dog ran
around the backyard chasing a butterfly.

when my friend got excited telling me the plot of
her favorite book.

and when my dad called me before i went to sleep
just to tell me he loved me.

maybe i'm not "falling" in love.
because i've done that before
and it just hurt.

maybe because every time i've *fallen* in love

i fell.

flat on my face
deep into a thorn bush.
cutting my skin wide open,
ripping me apart.

deep enough to scrape my heart.

that's what it took
for me to believe it was love.
to still love someone even after they take a knife
to your back.

i don't think i want to fall in love again.
i think i just want to love and be loved.

the same way i love the smile on my sister's face.
and the same way i love my best friends.

you don't need to fall first.
you can just love.
because sometimes when you fall first,
it's hard to want to stand back up again.

———

life after you

i forgive you.

i forgive you
for making me feel even lonelier while living in your presence,
than living in your absence.

i forgive you for every night i spent alone,
wondering if you were gonna call.

i forgive you for making me believe that a life after you would not exist.
and for every time i sat staring blankly into my childhood bedroom mirror,
with swollen eyes and a tired soul.

wondering
why i wasn't good enough.

i forgive you for the war you started within
my heart.

i forgive you for every time you battled me even after i threw up a white flag.
i forgive you for the ocean of salty tears i cried,
that had your name written all over it.

i've finally forgiven myself
for the addiction

life after you

i had to you.

i forgave myself for the self-abuse,
and for staying when i should have left.

i don't hate myself anymore.
i don't belittle myself for every promise
i believed.

and i don't think less of myself anymore
just because you could not be more.

so,
the last thing i have left to do
is
forgive you.

―――

life after you

i once read something that said

"women grieve after a breakup so they can glow later on, and how men bury their wounds in other women after a breakup so they don't have to cope with the loss of a love."

but it catches up to them eventually.

when the women stop coming through the revolving door.
that's when a man will truly begin to grieve the loss of the love they once had
with you.

that's when he starts to scroll through his instagram feed,
and finds a funny picture.

one that reminds him of you.

but when he tries sending it to you
the message fails.
because you are gone.

the ghost of you will follow him everywhere he goes.

it will follow him in the car

life after you

when that song comes on the radio.

or when he meets a girl with brown curly hair.

you will haunt him when someone asks him for a pinky promise.
and you will haunt him when he cracks a joke only you would have laughed at.

but the woman who stands before him cracks a smile and walks away.

just because it seems like you are the only one grieving.
doesn't mean it won't catch up to him *eventually*.

because he will look for parts of you in everyone he meets.
but he will never be able to find you.

and this will be your greatest form of revenge.

but hey.
i still hope you get everything you ever wanted,
i just hope i never hear a thing about it.

―――

life after you

a thank you letter to my ex.

i won't start this off with a list of things you did for me,
i'll start it off with the list of things you *didn't* do.

so thank you,
thank you for not showing up when i needed you.

thank you for forcing me to show up for myself.

thank you for reminding me that my heart is big and full of love.
even if i'm pouring every last drop of it into the wrong person, places, and things.

thank you for teaching me that loving the wrong person for so long
won't leave me broken.

it'll just leave me full, for a little while.
the pit in my stomach goes away after a while.

and then my body starts to crave the love you couldnt give me.
from other things,
like music, friends, and books.
thank you for reminding me that i was never as small as you painted me to be.

thank you for teaching me how to love, and feel.
even if the emotions i felt were not always happy.

they reminded me that i was still human,
and i was still soft.

and how the knives you threw at me
were never going to kill me.
because i was still able to bandage myself
back up.

which helped me prove to myself
that *i am not broken.*

there's a quote that says

"you wouldn't have learned how to ride a bike if someone you trusted hadn't let you go"

i've finally taken these training wheels off,
and i've never felt so free.

so thank you,
thank you for letting me go.

———

life after you

i thought i would live with a hole in my
heart forever.

i thought there would be an open wound.
one that only you knew how to bandage up.

i let it bleed for a while.
i let it hurt.
but then it healed.

not because you came back to bandage it up.
but because you were not the only person on
this planet
that could fix me.

———

life after you

no revenge, because one day in you're late
twenties you'll sit at your third bar of the night,
4 shots deep, talking to the 5th girl you saw walk
through the door.

you'll force small talk, and ask her what she wants
to be when she grows up.

she'll look at you and laugh because you are both
already grown.
and it's your first of many realizations that

it's too late.
you are too late.

no revenge, because her laugh will remind you
of mine.
and it all hits you at once.

the thoughts of what we could have been.
no revenge, because as you wobble out the door,
leaned up against a wall on the sidewalk, you will
scroll through your contact list and search for
my name.

it'll take you a second to find it
because your impaired vision and shaky hands
keep spelling my last name wrong.

life after you

no revenge, because after 10 minutes of scrolling
through your phone
you will find my number.
and click call.

no revenge, because i will let it ring.
again.
and again.
and again.

no revenge, because one day when your outside
that shitty bar
you will realize what you lost.

you will realize the girls, and the alcohol, and the
drugs, could never replace me.

no revenge because one day you will miss me.

when the revolving door of women just
isn't enough.

and you realize you are grown,
and everyone moved on.
you will miss me.
no revenge,
because my absence alone,

is the greatest revenge of all.

i don't pity the old me.

she was just a kid.
she grew up in a broken home,
mistaking love for abuse.

so how would she have known any different
at 16?

the whole time she was looking for the monster
under her bed.
no one told her
that the *monster* was the one
holding her hand
all along.

that 16-year-old girl still lives inside of me.

and i hug her every day.

———

life after you

i have let go of the idea
that it could have ended differently.

because if it was going to,
then it would have.

when i wish on stars, i don't wish for you
―――

life after you

i killed myself that day.

there was no funeral.
no flowers on my grave.
my friends did not create rivers from salty tears,
and they did not pray to the gods they believed in
for me to come back.

instead they all smiled.
i think for the first time in a while,
i smiled too.

and laughed.

there were balloons,
they threw a party,
and then there was cake.

i killed that version of me.
the one that i was with you.
i left her in the burning house.
the one you set on fire
before you walked away.

i probably could have followed you out the door.
tried to escape the fumes of smoke,
and chased you a little while longer.
but i didn't.
i let that version of me

life after you

die that day.

i laid her to rest
and let her sleep peacefully.

now i'm standing in the mirror
looking at myself.
this new version of me.
the one i gave birth to
all on my own.

i'm looking in the mirror
trying to forget what your arms looked like
wrapped around my torso.

traveling around me, like vines,
an invasive species.
slowing killing me
from the outside
making your way in.

i'm trying to forget,

but sometimes in my dreams
you're still suffocating me.

telling me, *your* vines are what make *me* beautiful.

but i wake up

life after you

and realize that girl is gone.

and she is never coming back.
and i'm no longer suffocating.

i've planted flowers
where your vines once grew.
that give me back my oxygen.
so now i can breathe.

your ghost may haunt me forever.

but the girl i killed that day
is never coming back.

―――

life after you

i wish you could see me now.
i don't straighten my hair anymore,
and i ditched the long sleeve shirts.
i stopped biting my nails,
and i got a new car.
i gave up my bad habits

the first one being you.

and i started wearing my retainer.
i put down the razor blades
and started going to therapy.

i'm no longer a danger to the people around me,
and i'm no longer a danger to myself.

you still cross my mind
when that song comes on the radio,
but it doesn't sting anymore.

i've grown up,

and i've outgrown
you.

i never thought it to be true,
but the grass is greener on this side.

i see life in color.

life after you

now that
i don't have
you.

―――

life after you

i wasn't made for one-night-stands.
they leave me abandoned and lonely.
i wasn't made for late-night drives in the dark
and kisses
behind closed doors.
i wasn't made for ubers home alone
and the half-hearted "see you around"

i was made to be seen,
loved,
touched,
praised.
i was made for love.
i was made for
"i'll love you with the light on"

i was made for
"text me when you get home"

i was made for
people
who are open to love,
not people who are afraid of it.

i hate pretending to be petrified of love
when it's what i crave.
craving long drives,
singing our favorite songs,
and laughing the whole way home.

life after you

i won't pretend to be cold with a heart made of ice
just so i don't get hurt.
i'd rather be burned alive.

i want to know that when my heart beats for the
last time
it was full of love.

i was full of love.

one day none of us are going to be here anymore,
and all you will leave on this planet
is the love you gave to others.

so maybe
one day
someone will realize
that *love*
is what i was made for.

―――

life after you

i did it.
that thing i told you i was going to do
all those years ago
well
i did it.

and my clothes are not cemented to the floor anymore.
they are on hangers in my closet.

and i don't flinch
when people reach above my knees
to get something from the glove compartment.
i.
don't.
flinch.

and i don't feel small anymore.
i don't feel lost.
i don't feel unseen.

i moved mountains.
and i set fire to the city.
i made noise.
i made magic.

i always had it in me.

i am more

than
broken
fucking
glass.

and i always was.
―――

life after you

"i miss you."
the first notification i wake up to
from the night before
it's 8 am on a sunday.

i can smell the liquor on your breath through
the screen
and your bitter longing
for something more
than a one-night-stand.

you buried your grief in a bottle of liquor
and saturdays with your friends.
while you left me to try and love the parts
of myself
you made me think were unlovable.

now all of a sudden at 4:12 in the morning
you think i'm gonna pick up the phone?
you think i'm gonna put my plans on pause
and run back to you?
just because you called?

you don't get to come back anymore.

i found love *after you*.
first within myself, after picking my own pieces
up off the floor.
and putting the mess you made back

life after you

together again.
and then with someone else.
who doesn't make me wonder
if he's gonna punch the walls today
or me.

who doesn't make me feel small,
or like a burden.
who doesn't keep me locked in a cage
hidden from the rest of the world.

i met someone who makes me question

why
i *ever* loved you.

it only took me learning
to love myself first.
for me to realize that.

you don't get to "miss me" anymore
―――

life after you

standing beside my mailbox,
i skim through the letters scattered inside.
i glance twice at a white envelope
a fairly bigger envelope than the rest.

no return address, just my name.
a punch to my gut
when i notice it's written in cursive.

i don't need a return address
to know it's from you.

i waited 457 days for this letter.
and one year ago was the last day i sat
by the mailbox waiting for it to come.

gaslighting myself into thinking it got lost
in the mail.
or you put the wrong zip code.

but now i hold it in my hands.

this letter is on fire,
but my hands have never felt this cold.

i walk it towards the garbage
and rip it between my fingers
leaving the envelope sealed.

i've put bandages on these wounds
i've cared for them
and let them heal.

i will *not* open this letter.
i will *not* reopen this wound.

let this letter die with the old version of me
___

life after you

you deserve love and kindness
you don't deserve to wonder.

you deserve to be touched gently
carried like an egg
forbidden to crack.

understand, that when a person
continues to shove the words "i love you"
down your throat

but their actions prove the opposite.
you will eventually choke.

so spit the words out.
and walk away.

dear the old me,

―――

if today you didn't make your bed
and all you ate was junk food.
or you did not eat at all.

if you thought you were over it
but caught yourself thinking about them
on your long drive home from work.

do not punish yourself.

sometimes healing feels like
climbing a spiral staircase.
you think you're moving in
a never-ending circle,

but really
you are just moving upward.

climb them at your own pace
___

life after you

and with all the bricks
that were thrown at me
head first.

i remained gentle,

despite it all.

―――

life after you

dear you,
i'm glad i loved you.
i'm glad i let you dig through my insides
and take my heart with you.
i'm glad you wore it as a gold star
for your own validation.

i'm happy our paths crossed–
you showed me all of the things
i never deserved.
and now i can search for the things i do.

loving you was never a waste.
i'll never forget you.
i'll never forget the paths i took
that led me to
the top of this mountain.

i never thought i'd get here.
maybe i'd give up on the way.
or take the wrong path.

but i finally made it.
and the view is great.

now that i have reached the top,
you are no longer in my line of sight.

life after you

it's peaceful here.

i think i'll stay a while

———

the recipe for getting over a lover

step 1: don't.
whoever tells you it's that easy,
and that you can just walk away,
has never been in love before.
and you wouldn't take baking advice from
someone who has never baked a cake before.
right?

step 2: cry.
until your pillow is wet
and you have to hang it to dry.
until your room is nothing but a puddle
full of fish that are his favorite color.

step 3: don't post the photo on instagram.
he knows you're pretty, he just doesn't love you.
so save it to your drafts for later.

step 4: go outside.
i know you feel superglued to your bed,
but he was not your oxygen.
go breathe near the trees.

step 5: cry again.

step 6: your friends will be your biggest savior.
go out on weekends
and have an occasional wine wednesday.
if you do not believe in a god,
believe he exists among your friends,
you will have them to thank eventually.

step 7: sit alone by the beach. once a week.
you can be your own girlfriend.
and one day you will realize
that is enough.

step 8: be kind
to yourself, to the people around you.
remember this is your first time on earth
and everyone else's first time too.

who knows,
the girls parked next to you at the beach
might also be grieving someone
who is still alive too.

―――

there was a time in my life
i didn't think i would make it.

i wanted to give up, and throw my life away,
because it was so scary thinking about navigating
a life
without you in it.

you were my lifeline, my oxygen,
you owned parts of my soul.

our hearts grew as one,
and i thought we would forever be interlinked.

but one day i woke up,
the sun still came up.
the birds still sat on my porch.
while singing their silly little songs.
and my favorite song
still played on the radio.

you promised to love me
until the day the earth stopped spinning.
and i promised i wouldn't live a life
that didn't have you in it.

i guess some promises *are* meant to be broken.
because there was life.

life after you

and it was beautiful.
and scary.
but gentle.

it taught me strength when i was weak.
and taught me patience when i was suffering.

i built this life for myself.
my life.

the life after you.

———

acknowledgements

i would like to thank my close friends for encouraging me to chase my dreams regardless of how big or small they might be, and being my rock throughout my journey in the poetry space. i would specifically like to thank Gianna Irizarry, Nicole Geres, Grace Giampaolo, Katie Magee, Lola Revasz, Sydney Vose and Kate Bulger for continuously listening to my ideas, giving me feedback on projects and being my go to support system. i have encountered many challenges within this past year, and would not have been able to navigate them without you all helping me along the way. your belief in me has provided the strength i needed to keep going, especially during moments of doubt. each of you has played an important part of my journey, reminding me that vulnerability can be a source of power. this book would not be possible if it wasn't for all of you. thank you.

to my readers

a message for those who listen to hayley grace.

i started writing poetry in my bedroom at age 13, reading them aloud into voice memos on my phone. never in a million years would that teenage girl believe her words would eventually impact people all across the world. a little girl's dream became a reality all because of you. to my readers, my followers, my listeners, all of my thanks goes out to you. i posted my first spoken poem in july of 2023. i did not expect anyone to see it as i had a total of 31 followers. the next morning i checked my phone and saw that my 31 followers had turned into 500 overnight. every single view, like, and comment gave me the motivation i needed to continue posting. for the very first time i had felt seen, heard, and that i finally had a voice. if you're reading this, you have changed my life and given me a platform so that i can hopefully change your life too. thank you for giving me the courage to disturb the comfortable, and comfort the disturbed. and thank you for letting me share my vulnerability with all of you. my writing isn't just speaking for me, but for the people who don't have the ability to share their own. i could not be more grateful for the opportunity all of you have given me.

also by the author

save me an orange

in *save me an orange*, hayley gives voice to the roots of struggle and pain growing up, as well as the love and pursuit of self-acceptance that were fundamental in her own choice to live. her verses weave a narrative that is both deeply personal and universally resonant–through shadows of the past and the fleeting moments of joy captured in the simplicity of sharing an orange.

"even when you think there's nothing left life gives us oranges
so go share one with your best friend
maybe they thought the world would end when they were 16 too."

-- from *save me an orange*

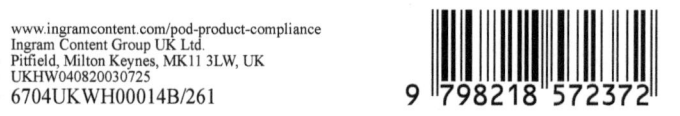

www.ingramcontent.com/pod-product-compliance
Ingram Content Group UK Ltd.
Pitfield, Milton Keynes, MK11 3LW, UK
UKHW040820030725
6704UKWH00014B/261